Martin Luther King Jr.

Terry Barber

ACTIVIST
SERIES

Martin Luther King Jr. is published by
Grass Roots Press, a division of Literacy Services of Canada Ltd.

PHONE 1–888–303–3213
WEBSITE www.literacyservices.com

ACKNOWLEDGEMENTS

We acknowledge the financial support of the Government of Canada through the Book Publishing Industry Development Program (BPIDP) for our publishing activities.

We acknowledge the support of the Alberta Foundation for the Arts for our publishing programs.

Editor: Dr. Pat Campbell
Image Research: Dr. Pat Campbell
Book design: Lara Minja, Lime Design Inc.

Library and Archives Canada Cataloguing in Publication

Barber, Terry, date
    Martin Luther King / Terry Barber.

(Activist series)
ISBN 1–894593–47–2

    1. King, Martin Luther, Jr., 1929–1968. 2. African Americans—
Biography. 3. Civil rights workers—United States—Biography. 4. Baptists—
United States—Clergy—Biography. 5. African Americans—Civil rights—
History—20th century. 6. Readers for new literates. I. Title. II. Series.

E185.97.K5B36 2006   323.1196'073092   C2006–902608–4

Printed in Canada

Contents

Martin Luther King Jr. is shot.

His friends point to the killer.

King is Shot

It is April 4, 1968. A 39-year-old man talks to his friends. His name is Martin Luther King Jr. His friends hear gunfire. A bullet hits King in the neck. King falls down. He dies one hour later.

King is shot in Memphis, Tennessee.

Coretta at her husband's funeral, April 9, 1968.

King is Shot

King leaves behind his wife, Coretta.
King leaves behind four children.
King leaves behind a world made sad
by his death.

More
than 50,000
people go to
King's funeral.

These people march for civil rights in 1963.

Segregation

The U.S. Civil War ends in 1865. The Civil War ends slavery. Martin Luther King Jr. is born in 1929. Black people are still not free. They do not have the same rights as white people.

Before the Civil War, slavery was legal in 15 states.

These people march to stop **segregation** in schools.

Segregation

In the South, most public places are segregated. There are laws to keep black and white people apart. Black and white people cannot go to the same school. They cannot eat together. A black and a white person cannot marry. They cannot even drink from the same water tap.

These black children live in the poor part of town.

Segregation

In the U.S., many black people are treated like second-class citizens. Black people live in the poor part of town. They have the worst jobs. Black people are paid less than white people for the same work. King is born into this world.

King was born in this house on January 15, 1929.

Early Years

Martin Luther King's father is a Baptist pastor. King's mother stays at home. She raises three children. King has a good home life. There is much love in his home.

Martin has one sister and one brother.

King listens to a speaker at his college.
King is third from left.

Early Years

King is very smart. He goes to school. He gets his **Ph.D.** King studies religion. King reads many books. These books change how King thinks. He learns that violence cannot solve problems.

Martin and Coretta King

Early Years

King falls in love and marries Coretta Scott. They live in Boston. In 1954, King takes a job in Montgomery, Alabama. King and his wife move to the South.

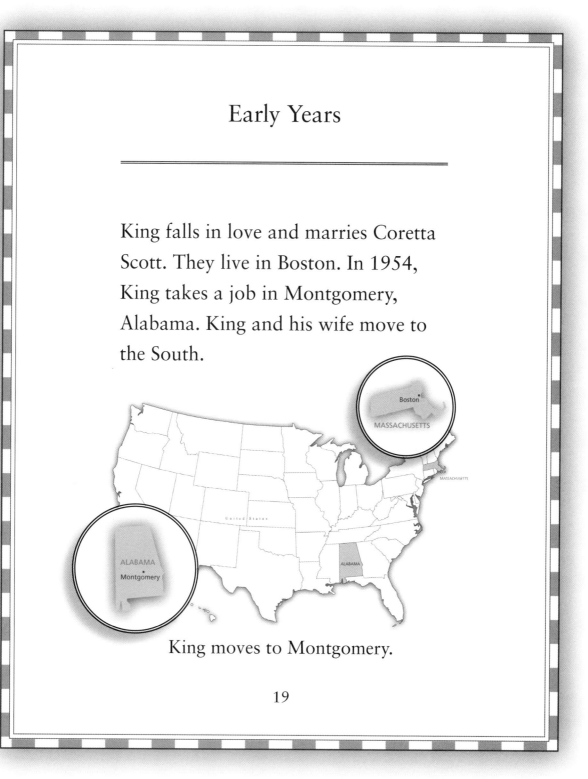

King moves to Montgomery.

King gives a sermon.

Early Years

King preaches at a Baptist church. His church is always full. People love to hear his sermons. King's **sermons** give people hope.

The police arrest Rosa Parks.

The Montgomery Bus Boycott

In 1955, the police arrest a black woman. Her crime? She will not give up her bus seat to a white person. Black leaders start a bus **boycott.** They ask Martin Luther King Jr. to lead the boycott. The boycott is a way to say segregation is wrong.

Rosa Parks will not give up her seat.

King rides the bus. He can choose where to sit.

The Montgomery Bus Boycott

Black people do not ride the buses for 381 days. The bus company loses money. In 1956, the blacks get their way. The U.S. Supreme Court rules that segregation on buses is wrong. Black people can choose where to sit. The boycott makes King famous.

This man takes the segregation sign off the bus.

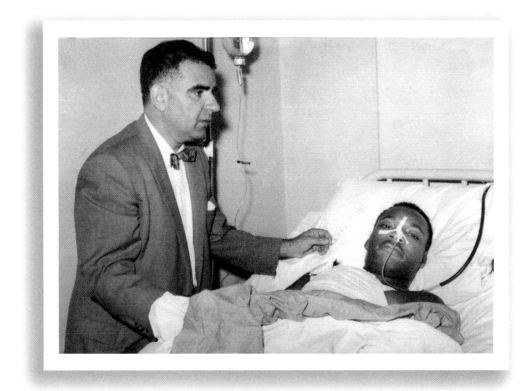

King gets stabbed. He goes to the hospital.

The Civil Rights Movement

Martin Luther King Jr. is a leader in the **civil rights movement.** Some people do not like King. He gets hate letters. He gets death threats. He gets stabbed.

The civil rights movement starts in the late 1950s.

King goes to jail.

The Civil Rights Movement

King believes peace is the way to
change the world. He believes in
nonviolence. He gives speeches.
He plans marches. He joins sit-ins.
Sometimes, he goes to jail for taking
part in these protests.

King gives his "I have a dream" speech.

The Civil Rights Movement

King gives speeches about equal rights.
His most famous speech is called
"I have a dream." He dreams of better
jobs for black people. He dreams of
better housing. He dreams of better
education.

King gives his famous speech to over 250,000 people.

These men take part in a sit-in.

The Civil Rights Movement

In the South, blacks cannot get a meal in some eating places. They cannot choose where to sit. Black people use sit-ins to **protest** segregation. The first sit-in takes place in 1960.

By 1961, 27 cities **ban** segregation in eating places. Black people can sit where they like.

Police attack the black marchers.

The Civil Rights Movement

King leads marches for freedom. Sometimes, the police attack the marchers. People see the attacks on TV. People see how blacks are treated. The U.S. President goes on TV. He talks about the need for civil rights.

President Johnson signs the 1964 Civil Rights Act.
King stands behind the President.

New Laws

The South begins to change. Black people get more rights. In 1964, the U.S. President signs the Civil Rights Act. This law says that segregation is not legal. Now, black and white people use the same public places.

King wins the Nobel Peace Prize in 1964.

This is the first day of the five-day march.

New Laws

In March 1965, Martin Luther King Jr. leads a march for voting rights. About 25,000 people take part in the march. The people march for five days. Later that year, the President signs the Voting Rights Act. This law makes it easier for black people to vote.

This map shows the five-day march. The march starts in Selma and ends in Montgomery.

This is a 1967 riot in New Jersey.

New Laws

By 1965, black people have more rights. But, racism is still a big problem across the U.S. In some cities, people start to riot. They are angry because jobs are hard to find. They are angry because they live in slums. King works hard to make life better for blacks.

These people are singing on Martin Luther King Day.

Free At Last

Martin Luther King Jr. helps to change how black people are treated all over the U.S. Today, black people have better jobs. Black and white children can go to the same school. Black people can vote without fear. King helps us all in his short life.

Martin Luther King day is a national holiday in the U.S.

Free At Last

The words "Free At Last" are on King's gravestone. He believed in freedom and equal rights. He changed how people, both black and white, look at the world. He made the world a better place for all people.

Picture Credits